THE BEST 50

CHILI RECIPES

Christie Katona
Thomas Katona

BRISTOL PUBLISHING ENTERPRISES
San Leandro, California

Printed in the United States of America.

ISBN 1-55867-130-7

Cover design: Paredes Design Associates
Cover Photography: John A. Benson
Food stylist: Suzanne Carreiro

ABOUT CHILI AND CHILE PEPPERS

Chili started out as a hot stew served to cowboys on the cattle trail in Texas. The flavor of the stew was enhanced by adding either fresh or dried chile peppers and other seasonings. Today, the variety of chilies, chili ingredients and preparation methods is almost endless.

The appreciation of a good bowl of chili is no longer restricted to "true" Southwesterners. The popularity of chilies and foods cooked with chile peppers has exploded in recent years due to the promotion of Southwestern cooking on television, and the availability of ingredients and good books on the subject.

CHILE PEPPERS

There are more than 140 varieties of chile peppers grown in the Southwestern United States and Mexico. Some are very hot and others are sweet and mild. The hotness of the chile is in the ribs or veins, and the seeds are hot due to their proximity to the veins. When the chile is cut in half, yellow or orange veins are an indication that the chile will be

a potent one. The oil in the chile, capsaicin, can cause severe burns, so never touch your face or eyes when handling hot chiles. Some people with sensitive skin wear rubber gloves. It also helps to handle chiles under running water. Use a small, sharp knife or a serrated grapefruit spoon to remove ribs, veins and seeds from chiles. If by chance you eat a chile that's far too hot for your comfort, milk is a great soother.

The following list provides a brief guide to chile peppers:

Anaheim is also known as "green chile." It is light to medium green and is long and slender (4 to 8 inches in length). It ranges from mild to medium in hotness and is sold fresh, canned or dried. For most uses, the fresh anaheim chile must be roasted to remove the tough peel and to soften the flesh. It is a very good, general-purpose chile.

Ancho is one of the most widely used chiles in Mexico. The fresh chile resembles a bell pepper but is tapered. When left to ripen, it turns a bright red. When dried, it is reddish brown in color and is wrinkled like a prune. It has a mild, sweet flavor.

Caribe is a crushed, dried, red chile, often seen in pizza parlors. The flavor improves when heated.

Cascabel is a round, rust-brown chile, about 1 to 2 inches in diameter. It has a nutty, sweet flavor and loose seeds. It is often available dried.

Chipotle is a chile often sold canned as "chipotle en adobo" (in adobo sauce). It is used mostly as a condiment, much like Tabasco Sauce.

Fresno is about 2 inches long and 1 inch in diameter. It is bright green in color and changes to orange and red when it matures. It is often canned or bottled and labeled as "hot chile pepper."

Habañero is the hottest chile of all, up to 1000 times hotter than a jalapeño. When used in Caribbean cuisine, it is often called a "Scotch bonnet." Due to its extreme heat, it is not readily available.

Jalapeño is a small, fat pepper (about 1 to 3 inches long) that ranges from dark green to bright green and from hot to very hot. It has a sharp and distinctive flavor and is probably the most well know pepper to those outside the Southwest. It is also sold pickled and sliced.

Pasilla ranges from 7 to 12 inches in length and is about 1 inch in diameter. It is dark green and turns to a dark brown as it matures.

Pimiento is available canned in the United States. It is heart- shaped, softer and sweeter than the common red bell pepper.

Poblano is a dark green wedge-shaped chile that is 5 to 6 inches long with a thick leathery skin. It ranges from medium to hot and has a complex flavor which is highly regarded in the Southwest and Mexico.

Serrano is smaller and considerably hotter than a jalapeño, but with a sweet edge. It is about 1 inch in length and ranges in color from green to orange to red. It is also sold in cans and jars and pickled.

Yellow wax (chiles güero) is slightly larger than a jalapeño, with about the same hotness. It is a slender, tapered chile ranging from 4 to 6 inches in length.

OTHER CHILI INGREDIENTS

Cilantro is the fresh,young, leafy plantlet of the herb coriander. It has a pungent, fresh flavor. *Coriander* is the dried seed of the cilantro plant.

Cumin is indigenous to the Southwest and Mexico, and comes in seeds and powder. For more flavor, toast the seeds and grind them yourself.

Oregano is highly aromatic with a pungent flavor that complements chili. Most oregano is the Italian variety. Mexican oregano is stronger. Crush regular dried oregano before using it to bring out the flavor.

HOT! HOT! HOT! CHILI

This is not for the faint of heart.

1 lb. hot Italian sausages
1 lb. sweet Italian sausages
¼ cup olive oil
2 cups chopped onions
6 cloves garlic, minced
6 jalapeño chiles, chopped
2 cans (28 oz. each) whole
  tomatoes, with juice
1 can (6 oz.) tomato paste

1 cup dry red wine
¼ cup chili powder
3 tbs. ground cumin
1 tbs. Tabasco Sauce
1 tbs. crumbled dried oregano
2 tsp. salt
2 tsp. fennel seeds
2 cans (15 oz. each) black
  beans, rinsed and drained

Cut sausages into 1-inch lengths. In a large soup kettle over medium high heat, cook sausages in olive oil until browned. Pour off all but 2 tbs. drippings. Add onion, garlic and jalapeños and cook until softened. Add remaining ingredients, except beans, and bring to a boil. Reduce heat, cover and simmer for 1 hour. Add beans and heat.

Makes 8-10 servings

HOT AND SPICY CHILI WITH OLIVES

When using canned beans, rinse them in a strainer with cold water, which will give them a fresher appearance and flavor. Taste as you go, adding spices to please your personal palate.

3 lb. boneless chuck, cut into ½-inch cubes
3 tbs. olive oil
½ cup hot chili powder
2 cups chopped onions
10 cloves garlic, minced
1 can (28 oz.) whole tomatoes, with juice
1 can (8 oz.) tomato sauce
1 can (6 oz.) tomato paste
1 cup dry red wine
1 can (16 oz.) dark red kidney beans, rinsed and drained
1 can (7-8 oz.) whole jalapeño chiles, chopped
2 tbs. brown sugar
1 tbs. freshly ground pepper
1 tbs. ground cumin
1 tbs. crumbled dried oregano

2 tsp. cinnamon
1 tsp. nutmeg
2 tsp. red pepper flakes
1 tsp. cayenne pepper
1 tsp. Worcestershire sauce
1 tsp. Tabasco Sauce
2 cups sliced ripe olives

Brown beef cubes in oil in a large soup kettle over medium high heat. Add chili powder, onions and garlic and cook until softened. Add remaining ingredients, except olives. Bring to a boil, reduce heat and simmer for 2 to 3 hours or until meat is very tender. Taste and correct seasoning. Add olives and heat through.

Makes 8 servings

SPEEDY TEX MEX CHILI

Chili con carne originated in the U.S., but it wasn't long before the Mexicans fell in love with it. This version goes together quickly.

2 lb. lean ground beef
1 cup chopped onion
2 cloves garlic, minced
1 can (28 oz.) whole tomatoes,
  with juice
¼ cup chili powder
1 tbs. ground cumin
1 tsp. salt

1 tsp. cayenne pepper
1 cup salsa
1 pkg. (10 oz.) frozen corn, thawed
1 can (15 oz.) pinto beans,
  rinsed and drained
8 green onions, sliced
sour cream and grated cheddar
  cheese for garnish

In a large soup kettle over medium high heat, brown ground beef, onion and garlic until beef is crumbly. Drain off excess juices. Add tomatoes, seasonings and salsa. Bring to a boil, reduce heat and simmer for 30 minutes. Add corn, beans and green onions and cook for 15 minutes. Serve with sour cream and grated cheddar.

Makes 8 servings

CHUCKWAGON BBQ CHILI

Use any commercially prepared barbecue sauce of your choosing to give this recipe your own signature.

2 lb. round steak, cut into ½-inch cubes
2 tbs. vegetable oil
1 cup chopped onion
1 cup chopped celery
1 cup chopped green bell pepper
3 cloves garlic, minced
1 can (16 oz.) whole tomatoes, with juice

1 can (12 oz.) beer
1 cup barbecue sauce
2 tbs. chili powder
1 tsp. crumbled dried oregano
1 tsp. salt
½ tsp. pepper
2 cans (15 oz. each) red kidney beans, rinsed and drained

In a large soup kettle over medium high heat, brown beef in oil. Add onion, celery, green pepper and garlic and cook until soft. Add remaining ingredients and bring to a boil. Reduce heat, cover and simmer for 2 hours or until meat is tender.

Makes 8 servings

CACTUS CHILI

*Look for the little leaves of the prickly pear cactus, called nopalitos,
canned or in jars in the Mexican foods section of your grocery store.*

5 strips bacon, chopped
1 tbs. olive oil
2 cups chopped onion
2 tsp. minced fresh garlic
2 jalapeño chiles, stemmed and minced
2 lb. beef chuck, cut into 1/2-inch cubes
1/2 cup mild chili powder
4 cups beef broth
1 cup dry red wine
1 cup crushed tomatoes
1 jar (10 oz.) roasted red peppers, coarsely chopped
2 cans (16 oz. each) pinto beans, rinsed and drained
1 jar (8 oz.) nopalitos, rinsed, drained and chopped

In a heavy soup kettle, cook bacon in oil until crisp. Drain bacon on paper towels and set aside. In drippings, brown onion, garlic and jalapeños until softened, about 10 minutes. Add beef and cook, stirring often, until it is browned. Stir in chili powder and cook for 5 minutes. Add broth, red wine and tomatoes and bring to a boil. Reduce heat, cover and simmer for 2 hours. Stir in roasted red peppers, beans, nopalitos and bacon; heat through.

Makes 8 servings

CHILI CON CARNE COLORADO

This simple chili is New Mexico style — simply red chile pods and cubed pork — and a very potent dish it is indeed! If you'd like, add canned black beans to this chili. In this recipe you make your own chile puree from scratch. Make a double batch of the puree and refrigerate it for up to 3 days, or freeze it.

1/4 lb. dry red chile pods
1 1/2 cups water
3 tbs. olive oil
2 cups chopped onion
2 tsp. minced garlic
2 1/2 lb. pork butt, cut into 1/2-inch cubes
1 tsp. ground cumin
1 tsp. crumbled dried oregano
1 1/2 tsp. salt
4 cups chicken broth
1 tsp. pepper

Remove stems from chiles. Cut them open with scissors and remove seeds. Rinse with cold water and cut them into 1-inch pieces. Bring water to a boil and pour it over chiles in a bowl. Cover and let cool. Drain water from chiles and reserve. Transfer softened chiles to the workbowl of a food processor and process to make a smooth puree. If necessary, add a bit of reserved liquid. Strain pureed chile mixture through a sieve to remove any seeds or bits of peel: you should have 1½ cups of puree.

In a large kettle, heat olive oil and sauté onion and garlic until softened. Add pork and cook until browned. Add chile puree and seasonings; cook for 5 minutes, stirring. Add chicken broth and bring to a boil. Lower heat and cover. Simmer for 2 hours or until meat is tender and sauce is thickened. Add salt and pepper to taste.

Makes 4-6 servings

NORTH TEXAS-STYLE RED CHILI

Decrease the amount of chili powder if this beanless chili is too wild for you! Gebhardt's is a nationally recognized brand.

4 lb. beef chuck, cut into ½-inch cubes
2 tbs. olive oil
1 can (10¾ oz.) beef broth
2 cups chopped onion
3 cloves fresh garlic, minced
4 jalapeño chiles, stemmed, seeded and minced

¼-½ cup Gebhardt's chili powder, to taste
2 tbs. cumin
1 tsp. crumbled dried oregano
1 can (16 oz.) tomato sauce
salt to taste
cayenne pepper tp taste

In a large soup kettle over medium high heat, brown beef in olive oil, stirring constantly. Add beef broth to cover meat. If necessary, add water to make enough liquid. Add chopped onion and simmer for 30 minutes. Stir in remaining ingredients, lower heat, cover and simmer for 3 hours or until meat is tender.

Makes 12 servings

QUICK CHILI

This recipe goes together in a flash. If you think of it, make it a day or two ahead and refrigerate it. The flavor mellows and becomes even better. Kids like this recipe, as it is less spicy than most and appeals to younger palates.

2 tbs. vegetable oil
2 lb. ground sirloin
2 cups chopped onion
2 cans (28 oz. each) plum
  tomatoes, with juice
1 cup beef broth

1 tbs. brown sugar
1 tbs. cider vinegar
1/2-3/4 cup mild chili powder
4 cans (16 oz. each) chili or
  pinto beans, rinsed and drained
salt to taste

In a large soup kettle, brown beef and onion in oil. Stir in remaining ingredients and simmer for 30 minutes. Add beans and heat through.

Makes 10 servings

EIGHT BEAN CHILI

Feel free to use any or all of these beans. This is a huge recipe for a crowd, so make sure you have a big enough soup kettle - or two! To toast coriander seeds, place them in a skillet over high heat and cook, stirring constantly until toasted. Grind them in a mini blender or use a mortar and pestle. You can find #10 cans of tomatoes in large warehouse clubs or restaurant supply stores.

$1/4$ lb. of each of the following 8 beans:

| kidney | pink | red | cranberry |
| white | black | pinto | navy |

Soak overnight in water to cover. The next day, drain and add fresh water to cover. Simmer for $1^1/_2$ hours or until beans are tender.

1 lb. bacon, diced
5 cups chopped onion
2/3 cup minced garlic
1/4 cup coriander seeds, toasted and ground
1 tbs.-1/4 cup cayenne pepper, or to taste
1/4 cup cinnamon

1/4 cup paprika
1/2 cup ground dried chile peppers
1 can (#10 size=108 oz.) plum tomatoes, with juice
12 oz. beer
5 lb. ground beef
salt and pepper to taste

While beans are simmering, in a large skillet over medium high heat, cook bacon until it begins to crisp. Add onion and garlic and sauté until softened. Stir in spices and ground chiles and cook for 5 minutes. Add tomatoes and beer and simmer for 30 minutes. In another large kettle, cook ground beef over medium high heat until crumbly. Drain off juices. Add tomato mixture to beef. Check beans to make sure they are tender. Add to meat/tomato mixture. Add salt and pepper. Cover and simmer for 1 hour.

Makes 25 servings

LAMB AND BLACK BEAN CHILI

Canned Italian plum tomatoes are ideal to use for chili recipes. Note the unusual seasonings and spices in this recipe — the sweet flavors of allspice and ginger complement the lamb.

1/4 cup olive oil
2 cups chopped onion
1 jalapeño chile, stemmed, seeded and minced
3 cloves garlic, minced
1 1/2 lb. ground lamb
2 tbs. chili powder
2 tbs. minced ginger root
2 tsp. dried thyme
1 tsp. crumbled dried marjoram
3/4 tsp. pepper
3/4 tsp. white pepper

3/4 tsp. cayenne pepper
3/4 tsp. allspice
2 cans (16 oz. each) plum tomatoes
1 1/2 cups dry red wine
2 cans (16 oz. each) black beans, rinsed and drained
salt to taste
1/2 cup sliced green onions for garnish
3 hard-cooked eggs, finely chopped, for garnish

Heat oil in a large kettle over medium high heat. Sauté onion,

jalapeño and garlic until they soften. Add lamb and cook until no longer pink, breaking up meat with a spoon, about 6 minutes. Add seasonings to meat and onion mixture. Cook for 5 minutes. Add tomatoes and wine. Cover and simmer for 30 minutes. Add beans and heat through. Serve in bowls sprinkled with sliced green onions and chopped hard-cooked egg, if desired.

Makes 8 servings

PORK AND BEEF CHILI

*Coffee adds richness to this good, meaty chili. To facilitate cutting
the meat, partially freeze it until it's ice cold. To seed a fresh tomato,
cut in half horizontally and gently squeeze over the sink.*

1 tbs. olive oil
2 lb. boneless pork, cut into
  ½-inch cubes
2 lb. boneless beef chuck, cut
  in ½-inch cubes
2 cups chopped onion
2 cloves garlic, minced
1 red bell pepper, diced
1 jalapeño chile, stemmed,
  seeded and minced
3 tbs. chili powder
2 tbs. ground cumin

2 tsp. salt
1 tsp. pepper
1 tsp. cayenne pepper
2 cups cooked red kidney beans
1½ cups cold brewed coffee
1 can (6 oz.) tomato paste
4 fresh tomatoes, seeded and
  chopped
shredded Monterey Jack cheese,
  sour cream, sliced avocado, and
  sliced green onions for garnish

In a large kettle over medium high heat, heat oil and sauté pork cubes for 15 minutes, stirring frequently. Add beef cubes and cook for an additional 20 minutes or until all meat is browned. Add onion, garlic and jalapeño and stir until softened. Add remaining ingredients. Bring to a boil and reduce heat to low. Simmer for 2 hours.

Makes 10 servings

GREEN TOMATO CHILI

This is just the recipe to make when your garden has an over-abundant supply of green tomatoes. Tomatillos are small, green, round fruits just a bit larger than a cherry tomato. They are enclosed in a brown paperlike husk. Be careful not to overcook them.

1/4 cup olive oil
3 lb. beef, ground for chili
3 cloves garlic, minced
1 cup chopped onion
6-8 anaheim chiles, stemmed,
  seeded and finely chopped

4 large green tomatoes, chopped
water as needed
3 tomatillos, husked and chopped
salt and pepper to taste
flour tortillas
sour cream and salsa for garnish

In a large kettle, heat oil over medium high heat and brown meat, stirring constantly. Add garlic and onion and cook until limp. Add chiles and green tomatoes. Add water to cover. Reduce heat, cover and simmer for 2 hours. Just before serving, add tomatillos, salt and pepper; heat through. Ladle into bowls and serve with tortillas, salsa and sour cream.

Makes 8-12 servings

CHORIZO CHILI

Chorizo is highly seasoned pork sausage of Mexican origin.

2 lb. chorizo sausage meat
1/4 cup olive oil
2 lb. beef chuck, cut into 1/2-inch
  cubes
3 cups chopped onion
2 tsp. chopped garlic
5 tbs. chili powder
1 tbs. crumbled dried oregano

2 tsp. ground cumin
2 tsp. salt
1 tsp. pepper
24 oz. beer
1 can (6 oz.) tomato paste
2 cans (28 oz. each) plum
  tomatoes, with juice, chopped

In a large skillet over medium high heat, brown chorizo, breaking it up with a metal spoon until cooked and crumbly. Drain off excess fat and liquid and set aside. In a large soup kettle, heat oil over medium high heat. Brown chuck in batches; do not crowd. When all beef is browned, return to skillet with chorizo. Add onion, garlic and spices; cook until onion is softened. Add beer, tomato paste and tomatoes. Bring to a boil, cover and reduce heat. Simmer for 3 hours.

Makes 8-12 servings

VENISON CHILI

If you have hunters in your family, this recipe will come in handy. Masa harina, which is fine cornmeal, is used to thicken the chili. For a change of pace, use ground pork instead of ground venison.

3 tbs. vegetable oil
1 cup chopped onion
2 cloves garlic, minced
1 jalapeño chile, stemmed,
 seeded and minced
1 lb. venison, cut into ½-inch
 cubes
1 lb. ground venison
1 can (28 oz.) crushed tomatoes,
 with juice
1 green bell pepper, chopped

3 tbs. red wine vinegar
3 tbs. chili powder
2 tsp. ground cumin
2 tbs. Worcestershire sauce
¾ tsp. cayenne pepper
2 tsp. salt
1 tsp. pepper
1 can (16 oz.) red kidney beans,
 rinsed and drained
3 tbs. masa harina
2 tbs. cold water

Heat oil in a large soup kettle over medium high heat. Add onion, garlic and jalapeño and cook until softened. Add cubed and ground venison and continue cooking until meat is no longer red, about 6 minutes. Add tomatoes, bell pepper, vinegar and seasonings. Bring to a boil and cover. Reduce heat to simmer and cook for 1 hour. Just before serving, add kidney beans. Combine masa harina with cold water to form a smooth paste. Stir into chili mixture and heat to thicken.

Makes 8 servings

CINCINNATI CHILI

This chili is legendary! It is served at restaurants throughout Cincinnati. It can be served over spaghetti, which is called 2-way Cincinnati chili; 3-way chili adds cheese, and 4-way adds chopped onion to the cheese. It is also served over a hot dog on a bun, topped with onions and cheese.

2 lb. ground beef
4 cups beef broth
1 tbs. olive oil
3 cups chopped onion
4 cloves garlic, minced
1/4 cup chili powder
1 tsp. ground cumin
1 tsp. cinnamon
1 tsp. celery seed
1 tsp. red pepper flakes

1 tsp. nutmeg
1 tsp. paprika
1 tsp. allspice
1/2 tsp. cloves
1 bay leaf
2 cups tomato sauce
2 tbs. red wine vinegar
1/2 oz. unsweetened chocolate
1 can (16 oz.) kidney beans,
  optional

In a heavy soup kettle over medium high heat, cook ground beef in beef broth 1 hour. Cool in the refrigerator and lift off fat. Place olive oil in a large skillet and sauté onion and garlic until softened. Combine onion mixture with beef and broth in soup kettle; turn heat to medium high. Add tomato sauce, vinegar and chocolate and simmer for 1 hour. Add canned kidney beans after the mixture is cooked if desired. Remove bay leaf and serve 1-way, 2-way, 3-way or 4-way!

Makes 8 servings

SOME LIKE IT HOT CHILI

Ancho chiles are dark brown and shaped like a triangle, and the most frequently used chile in Mexican cooking.

6 dried ancho chiles, seeded
water
2 cans (14 oz. each) tomatoes, with juice
1 cup beer
1 cup canned beef broth
¼ cup chili powder
2 tbs. ground cumin
2 tbs. paprika
2 tsp. crumbled dried oregano

1 tsp. sugar
3 tbs. vegetable oil
3 cups chopped onion
10 cloves garlic, minced
2 lb. beef chuck steak, cut into ½-inch cubes
¼ cup flour
⅛ tsp. cayenne pepper

Place ancho chiles in a small saucepan and cover with water. Bring to a boil, reduce heat and simmer for 15 minutes. Remove from heat and cool. With a food processor or blender, combine drained chiles, tomatoes, beer, beef broth, spices and sugar. Process until smooth and set aside.

In a large kettle, heat oil and sauté onion and garlic until tender but not brown. Remove onion mixture to a bowl and set aside. In the same kettle, add beef cubes and cook, stirring frequently, until light brown, about 10 minutes. Sprinkle with flour and stir well. Return onion mixture to kettle and stir in tomato spice mixture. Stir well and bring mixture to a boil. Reduce heat and simmer, covered, for 2 to 3 hours or until beef is very tender and sauce is thickened.

Makes 8 servings

LIMA BEAN AND SAUSAGE CHILI

*Use any type of Italian sausage you prefer in this recipe,
either hot or mild, or a combination of both.*

1½ lb. dried small lima beans
½ lb. bacon, cut into ½-inch pieces
2 tbs. olive oil
2 lb. Italian sausage, casings removed
3 cups chopped onion
3 cloves garlic, minced
3 tbs. chili powder
1 tbs. ground cumin
2 tsp. dry mustard
1 can (28 oz.) crushed tomatoes, with juice
⅓ cup red wine vinegar
2 tbs. Worcestershire sauce
1 tsp. salt
½ tsp. freshly ground pepper

Place limas in a large bowl, cover with water and soak overnight. Drain beans, cover with fresh water and bring to a boil. Add bacon, reduce heat and simmer until beans are very tender, about 2 hours. Drain, reserve cooking liquid.

In a large kettle, heat oil over medium high heat. Add sausage and cook until browned, breaking up with a spoon. Add onion and garlic and cook until softened. Add remaining ingredients and beans. Reduce heat to low and simmer for 1½ hours; add some reserved bean liquid if mixture becomes too dry.

Makes 12 servings

LAMB AND LENTIL CHILI

Garnish this dish with chopped cilantro. Cilantro is a pungent herb usually sold in bunches with the roots left on. It is also known as fresh coriander and Chinese parsley. Store it in the refrigerator upright in a jar of water with a plastic bag over the top and it will keep well for several days.

3 tbs. olive oil
2 cups chopped onion
3 cloves garlic, minced
2 tbs. chili powder
1 tbs. paprika
1 tbs. ground cumin
1 tsp. red pepper flakes
1 tsp. cayenne pepper
½ tsp. ground coriander
1 lb. ground lamb
1 cup dried red lentils

2 cups beef broth
1 can (14½ oz.) can crushed
  tomatoes, with juice
1 tbs. crumbled dried oregano
1 tsp. dried rosemary
1 tbs. salt
2 tsp. sugar
1 tsp. pepper
⅓ cup finely chopped cilantro
  for garnish

Heat oil in a large kettle over medium high heat. Sauté onion and garlic until softened. Add chile powder and spices, stirring for 2 minutes to develop the flavor. Add ground lamb and stir until cooked through and crumbly. Add lentils, broth, tomatoes and seasonings. Bring to a boil, reduce heat to low and simmer for 30 minutes or until lentils are tender. Add a bit of water if mixture becomes too dry. Ladle into serving bowls and garnish with cilantro.

Makes 6 servings

CHILI ITALIAN STYLE

Fennel, Italian sausage, balsamic vinegar and basil
add a bit of Italian flair to this recipe.

2 tbs. olive oil
1 cup chopped onion
2 cloves garlic, minced
1 cup chopped fennel bulb
1 fresh red chile pepper, seeded and minced
1 lb. hot Italian sausage, cut into ½-inch slices
1½ lb. skinless, boneless chicken thighs, cut into 1-inch chunks
1 cup chicken broth
1 can (16 oz.) crushed tomatoes in puree
1 can (6 oz.) tomato paste
1 tbs. balsamic vinegar
1 tbs. crumbled dried oregano
1 tbs. ground cumin
1 tbs. chili powder
4 fresh plum tomatoes, coarsely chopped

1 pkg. (10 oz.) frozen corn kernels, thawed
salt and pepper
sour cream for garnish
1/4 cup finely chopped fresh basil for garnish

Heat oil in a large soup kettle over medium high heat. Sauté onion and garlic until tender. Add fennel and chile and continue to cook until softened. Add sausages and cook for 10 minutes. Add chicken pieces and cook an additional 10 minutes. Spoon off all but 2 tbs. oil. Stir in chicken broth, tomatoes, tomato paste, vinegar and seasonings. Bring to a boil. Turn heat to low, cover and simmer for 30 minutes. Add corn, chopped tomatoes and season to taste with salt and pepper. Just before serving, top with sour cream and basil.

Makes 8 servings

SPICY TWO-BEAN CHILI WITH BEER

Grocery stores now carry a wide variety of special sausages. It's fun to experiment with the different combinations.

2 tbs. vegetable oil
2 large onions, chopped
1 red bell pepper, chopped
1 jalapeño chile, seeded
  and chopped
1 tbs. minced fresh garlic
1 tbs. chili powder
2 tbs. ground cumin
2 tbs. fresh dill
1 tbs. dried basil
1 tbs. crumbled dried oregano
1 tbs. paprika
1 tsp. pepper
2 lb. pork, cut into ½-inch cubes

2 lb. hot Italian sausage, cut into
  ½-inch lengths
1 can (15 oz.) black beans,
  rinsed and drained
1 can (15 oz.) red kidney beans,
  rinsed and drained
1 can (15 oz.) can diced tomatoes,
  with juice
1 can (6 oz.) tomato paste
1 cup salsa
1 cup beer
sour cream for garnish
grated cheddar cheese for garnish

In a large kettle, heat oil and sauté onions, red pepper, jalapeño and garlic until softened. Stir in spices and herbs. In a large skillet, cook sausage and pork cubes until sausage is well browned and pork cubes are cooked through. Drain off any excess fat. Add meat mixture to onion mixture. Add remaining ingredients and simmer for 2 hours. Season to taste with salt. Serve garnished with sour cream and grated cheddar.

Makes 8-10 servings

PORK PICADILLO CHILI

Picadillo typically refers to a sweet and spicy meat mixture common in Mexican cooking. It is used in enchiladas, burritos and tacos. This is a variation of the theme for chili.

1 lb. lean ground pork
1 cup chopped onion
2 cloves garlic, minced
1 can (28 oz.) whole tomatoes, with juices
1 can (6 oz.) tomato paste
1 can (16 oz.) red kidney beans, rinsed and drained
1 can (4 oz.) diced green chiles
2 tsp. ground cumin

1 tsp. chili powder
1/2 tsp. cinnamon
1 tsp. salt
1/2 tsp. pepper
dash Tabasco Sauce
1/3 cup dark seedless raisins
1/3 cup toasted slivered almonds
cooked white rice
sour cream for garnish
cilantro for garnish

In a large soup kettle over medium high heat, brown pork, onion and garlic until pork is cooked through and crumbly. Drain off any excess fat. Stir in tomatoes, tomato paste, beans, chiles and spices. Bring to a boil, reduce heat to low, cover and simmer for 30 minutes. Taste and correct seasoning. Serve over cooked rice and garnish with sour cream and cilantro.

Makes 8 servings

CHILI WITH MEAT

CHOOSE YOUR BEANS CHILI

There are many unusual varieties of dried beans available to experiment with when creating your own chili. Try Spanish tolosanos, Steuben yellow eyes, cranberry beans, tongues of fire and other types that spark your interest.

1 cup dried beans
2 tbs. vegetable oil
2 lb. beef, cut into 1-inch chunks
2 lb. ground pork
2 cups sliced green onions
12 cloves garlic, minced
5 cups beef broth
2 cans (4 oz. each) diced green
  chiles

2/3 cup chopped fresh cilantro
3 tbs. chili powder
1 tbs. crumbled dried oregano
1/8 tsp. cayenne pepper
2/3 cup yellow cornmeal
salt and black pepper to taste

Soak beans in water overnight. Drain beans, cover with fresh water and bring to a boil. Reduce heat and simmer for 1 hour or until tender. Heat oil in a soup kettle and brown beef and pork. Remove with a slotted spoon to a bowl. Brown green onions and garlic in pan drippings until soft. Add meat back to kettle and add 3 cups of the beef broth, cooked beans, green chiles, cilantro and seasonings. Simmer for 2½ hours. In remaining cup of broth, mix cornmeal and add to kettle. Reduce heat and cook until thickened, about 5 minutes.

Makes 8 servings

VEAL CHILI WITH BLACK BEANS

Cumin is available in both seeds and powdered form.

2 tbs. olive oil
1½ cups chopped onion
3 cloves garlic, minced
2 lb. veal for stew, cut into ½-inch
  cubes
1 can (28 oz.) whole tomatoes,
  with juice

1 cup water, or as needed
2 tbs. chili powder
1 tbs. ground cumin
1 tbs. unsweetened cocoa
salt to taste
1 can (15 oz.) black beans,
  rinsed and drained

Heat 1 tbs. of the olive oil in a heavy kettle over medium high heat and sauté onion and garlic until softened. In a large skillet, add remaining oil and brown veal over medium high heat. Add veal to onion mixture. Add tomatoes, chili powder, cumin and cocoa to kettle and bring to a boil over high heat. Add water to make sure liquid covers veal. Reduce heat, cover and simmer for 1 hour. Taste and correct seasoning adding salt as needed. Add beans and heat through, about 10 minutes.

Makes 8 servings

PORK AND BLACK BEAN CHILI

This makes a delicious topping for baked potatoes. Serve them with sour cream, shredded cheddar, diced red onion, avocado cubes and chopped cilantro.

1½ lb. boneless pork loin or shoulder, cut into ½-inch cubes
3 tbs. vegetable oil
1 cup chopped onion
2 cloves garlic, minced
2 tbs. chili powder
2 tsp. ground cumin
2 tsp. crumbled dried oregano
2 cans (16 oz. each) crushed tomatoes in puree
2 cans (16 oz. each) black beans, rinsed and drained
salt and pepper to taste

Heat oil in a large soup kettle over medium heat. Add pork and cook, stirring frequently, until pork is no longer pink. Add onion and garlic and cook until onion is softened and pork is browned. Stir in remaining ingredients and simmer for 30 minutes. If mixture becomes too thick, add water. Garnish as desired.

Makes 4 servings

CHILI WITH MEAT

HAM AND BLACK-EYED PEA CHILI

When fresh black-eyed peas are in season, this chili is a treat.

3 lb. black eyed peas, shelled
3 tbs. olive oil
2 cloves garlic, minced
1 cup chopped onion
3 anaheim chiles, stemmed,
seeded and minced
1 red serrano chile, stemmed,
seeded and minced
1 lb. ham, cut into ½-inch cubes

2 cans (16 oz. each) plum
tomatoes, with juice
¼ cup finely chopped cilantro
1 tbs. crumbled dried oregano
2 tsp. sugar
2 tsp. red wine vinegar
1 tsp. salt
cooked white rice

Bring a large kettle of water to a boil and add peas. Boil for 2 minutes, drain and rinse with cold water to stop the cooking. Set aside. Heat oil in a large kettle over medium high heat. Add garlic, onion and chiles and sauté until onion is soft. Add remaining ingredients and peas. Lower heat to medium and cook for 10 minutes, stirring often, until mixture is thickened and peas are tender. Serve over rice.

Makes 4-6 servings

CHICKEN CHILI VERDE

Chicken with green chiles is a light and flavorful chili.

2 lb. boneless chicken breasts,
  cut into 1-inch cubes
1 tbs. vegetable oil
2 cups chopped onion
3 cloves garlic, minced
2 jalapeño chiles, stemmed and
  seeded
1 tbs. ground cumin
1 tbs. crumbled dried oregano

2 tsp. red pepper flakes
2 cups chicken broth
2 cans (4 oz. each) diced green
  chiles
1 cup beer
1 can (16 oz.) tomatillos
salt and pepper to taste
$\frac{1}{4}$ cup chopped parsley
$\frac{1}{4}$ cup chopped cilantro

In a large soup kettle over medium high heat, cook chicken breasts in oil until light brown. Add onion, garlic and jalapeños and sauté until softened. Add cumin, oregano, red pepper flakes, chicken broth, chiles and beer. Bring to a boil, reduce heat and simmer for 1 hour. Add tomatillos, salt and pepper. Serve sprinkled with parsley and cilantro.

Makes 8 servings

BLACK AND WHITE CHILI

Black and white beans create this colorful chili.

2 tbs. olive oil
2 lb. boneless chicken breasts,
  cut into 1-inch chunks
1 cup chopped onion
3 cloves garlic, minced
2 red bell peppers, diced
3 tbs. chili powder
1 tbs. ground cumin
1 tbs. dried, crumbled oregano
1 tsp. red pepper flakes

2 cups tomato juice
1 can (6 oz.) tomato paste
1 can (28 oz.) whole tomatoes,
  with juice
1 can (15 oz.) black beans,
  rinsed and drained
1 can (15 oz.) cannellini beans,
  rinsed and drained
lime wedges, sour cream and
  cilantro for garnish

Heat oil in a large soup kettle over medium high heat. Cook chicken cubes until cooked through and beginning to brown, about 5 minutes. Add onion, garlic and peppers and cook until tender. Add remaining ingredients, bring to a boil and reduce heat. Simmer for 1 hour. Serve with lime wedges, sour cream and cilantro.

Makes 8 servings

WHITE BEAN AND CHICKEN CHILI

This is a good way to use up leftover chicken or turkey.

1 tbs. olive oil
1 onion, peeled and chopped
3 cloves garlic, minced
1 red bell pepper, chopped
2 cans (15 oz. each) white beans,
  rinsed and drained
1 can (4 oz.) diced green chiles
1 tsp. ground cumin
2 tsp. chili powder

1 can (14½ oz.) chicken broth
2 cups diced cooked chicken or
  turkey
2 tbs. lime juice
2 tbs. chopped cilantro
salt and pepper to taste
6 tbs. sour cream for garnish
6 tbs. salsa for garnish

In a large kettle over medium heat, sauté onion and garlic in olive oil until soften. Stir in beans, chiles, cumin, chili powder and broth. Bring to a boil, reduce heat and simmer for 10 minutes. Add chicken and cook 10 minutes longer. Stir in lime juice and cilantro. Add salt and pepper. Ladle into bowls and top with sour cream and salsa.

Makes 6 servings

CHICKEN CHILI WITH TEQUILA AND LIME

Tequila and lime add intriguing flavors to this dish.

3 tbs. olive oil
2 cups chopped onion
4 cloves garlic, minced
1 tbs. chili powder
1 tbs. ground cumin
1 tsp. red pepper flakes
1 tsp. ground coriander
1½ lb. ground chicken
1 can (28 oz.) crushed tomatoes
   with juice
2 tbs. tomato paste
½ cup tequila
¼ cup lime juice

¼ cup finely chopped fresh
   cilantro
1 tbs. dried crumbled basil
1 tbs. dried oregano
2 tsp. dried leaf savory
2 tsp. salt
1 tsp. pepper
2 bay leaves
1 tbs. sugar
2 tbs. masa harina
cooked white rice
cilantro sprigs for garnish
lime wedges for garnish

In a large soup kettle, heat oil over medium high heat. Add onion, garlic, chili powder, cumin, red pepper flakes and coriander. Cook until onions are softened. Add chicken and cook until no longer pink; break up meat with a spoon. Stir in tomatoes, tomato paste, tequila, lime juice and seasonings. Bring to a boil and reduce heat. Simmer, stirring occasionally, for 1¼ hours. Sprinkle with masa harina and simmer until thickened, about 15 minutes. Remove bay leaves. Serve over rice and garnish with cilantro and lime.

Makes 6 servings

CHILI BLANCO

Ground turkey and pink beans make this chili "new wave."

2 tbs. vegetable oil
1 lb. ground turkey
1 cup chopped onion
2 cloves garlic, minced
2 tbs. chili powder
2 tsp. ground cumin
1 tsp. crumbled dried oregano
salt and pepper
1 can (4 oz.) diced green chiles

1 can (16 oz.) crushed tomatoes
 in puree
1 can (16 oz.) chicken broth
1 can (16 oz.) pink kidney beans,
 rinsed and drained
sour cream, diced avocado,
 salsa, shredded cheddar
 cheese, cilantro and lime
 wedges for garnish

Heat oil in a large soup kettle over medium high heat. Cook turkey, onion and garlic until turkey is light brown and onion is soft. Drain off excess fat and juices. Add remaining ingredients and simmer for 30 minutes. Season to taste with salt and pepper. Garnish as desired.

Makes 6 servings

CHICKEN AND GARBANZO CHILI

Fresh ground chicken is readily available at your grocery store, and it's a healthier alternative to beef or pork.

1 lb. ground chicken
1 cup chopped onion
2 cloves garlic, minced
½ cup chopped bell pepper
1 can (28 oz.) whole tomatoes, with juice
1 can (4 oz.) diced green chiles
1 can (6 oz.) tomato paste
1 cup chicken broth

1 can (16 oz.) garbanzo beans, rinsed and drained
1 can (16 oz.) red kidney beans, rinsed and drained
2 tbs. chili powder
1 tsp. salt
1 tsp. sugar
1 tsp. ground cumin
¼ tsp. cayenne pepper

In a large soup kettle over medium high heat, sauté chicken, onion and garlic until chicken is cooked and crumbly. Drain off any excess juices. Add remaining ingredients, bring to a boil, reduce heat and cover. Simmer for 30 minutes, stirring occasionally.

Makes 6 servings

WHITE CHILI

This healthy, flavorful chili has many unusual ingredients.

1 cup chopped onion
½ cup finely chopped carrots
4 cloves garlic, minced
¼ cup olive oil
1 tbs. ground cumin
1 tsp. dried savory
1 lb. ground turkey
2 lb. boneless turkey breast, cut into ½-inch cubes
⅔ cup pearl barley

1 can (15 oz.) garbanzo beans, rinsed and drained
1 can (15 oz.) navy beans, rinsed and drained
1 can (4 oz.) diced green chiles
1 cup chicken broth
2 tbs. chopped fresh cilantro
1½ tbs. arrowroot dissolved in ½ cup water
salt and freshly ground pepper

In a large soup kettle over medium high heat, sauté onion, carrots and garlic in olive oil until softened. Add cumin, savory and turkey; cook until no longer pink. Add barley, beans, chiles, chicken broth and cilantro; simmer for 30 minutes, or until barley is tender. Stir in arrowroot mixture. Simmer, uncovered, for 15 minutes until thick. Season to taste.

Makes 6 servings

SEAFOOD CHILI

In this unusual recipe, the seafood is cooked separately from the seasoned bean mixture so that it doesn't overcook. Canned chipotle chiles are available wherever Mexican foods are sold.

3 tbs. olive oil
1 cup diced onion
3 cloves garlic, minced
1 cup diced green bell pepper
1 small jalapeño chile, seeded
  and minced
2 tsp. finely chopped chipotle
  chiles
1 tsp. ground cumin
1 tsp. chili powder
1 tsp. onion powder
1/2 tsp. crumbled dried oregano
1/2 tsp. salt
1 tsp. pepper

1 can (15 oz.) black beans
  rinsed and drained
1 cup chicken broth
1 can (28 oz.) diced tomatoes,
  with juice
1 1/2 lb. fish fillet, cut into 1/2-inch
  cubes (cod, sea bass or sole)
1 lb. bay shrimp
8 oz. shredded Monterey Jack
  cheese for garnish
1/4 cup chopped cilantro for garnish
1 cup salsa
6 flour tortillas, cut in half and
  rolled

Heat 1 tbs. of the oil in a large kettle over medium heat. Sauté onion, garlic, bell pepper, jalapeño, chipotle and seasonings for 5 minutes. Add beans, broth and tomatoes and reduce heat to low. Cover and simmer for 20 minutes.

Heat remaining olive oil in a skillet and sauté fish for 2 minutes, or until opaque. Add shrimp and heat through. Combine seafood with bean mixture and cook for an additional 2 minutes to blend flavors. Ladle into bowls and sprinkle with cheese and cilantro. Top with salsa and serve with flour tortillas.

Makes 6 servings

VEGETARIAN CHILI

If you prefer less crunchy vegetables, cook 20 to 30 minutes longer.

1/4 cup vegetable oil
1 cup chopped red onion
4 cloves garlic, minced
3 cans (16 oz. each) pinto beans,
  rinsed and drained
2 cups cauliflower florets
1 green bell pepper, diced
1 sweet potato, peeled and diced
2 carrots, peeled and diced
3 cups frozen corn

1 can (35 oz.) tomatoes,
  chopped, with juice
1 cup vegetable broth
1/4 cup tomato paste
3 tbs. ground cumin
3 tbs. chili powder
2 tsp. paprika
1 1/2 tsp. salt
1/8 tsp. cayenne pepper
1/4 cup chopped fresh cilantro

In a large soup kettle, heat oil and cook onion and garlic over medium heat until tender, but not brown. Add remaining ingredients to kettle and stir well. Bring to a boil, stirring frequently. Reduce heat to low and simmer, covered, for 15 minutes. Top with cilantro to serve.

Makes 8 servings

VEGETARIAN CHILI WITH CORN AND CHOCOLATE

*This chili is rich and substantial in spite of the fact it has no meat. Unsweetened chocolate is often found in chili recipes; it balances the tomatoes well and adds depth to the flavor. For an interesting change of pace, top the chili with **Avocado And Red Onion Relish**.*

¼ cup vegetable oil
3 cups chopped onion
2 tsp. minced fresh garlic
2 tbs. chili powder
1½ tbs. ground cumin
1 tbs. crumbled dried oregano
2 cans (28 oz. each) plum
  tomatoes, with juice
1-2 jalapeño chiles, stemmed
  and minced
1-2 cups water

2 red bell peppers, diced
3 cans (16 oz. each) red kidney
  beans, well drained
1 pkg. (10 oz.) frozen corn,
  thawed
1 square (1 oz.) unsweetened
  chocolate
salt to taste
water if necessary

In a large kettle, heat oil and sauté onion and garlic until limp. Sprinkle with seasonings. Add tomatoes, jalapeños, water and bell pepper and simmer for 20 minutes. Add beans, corn, chocolate and salt. Cook until beans are heated through and corn is tender. Add water if you wish a thinner chili. Pour chili into bowls and garnish with *Avocado And Red Onion Relish*.

Makes 8 servings

AVOCADO AND RED ONION RELISH

2 avocados, peeled and diced
1 red onion, chopped
3 tbs. fresh lime juice
2 tbs. olive oil

½ tsp. sugar
½ tsp. salt
½ cup chopped fresh cilantro

Combine all ingredients, cover and chill.

Makes 1½ cups

SUN-DRIED TOMATO CHILI

The meaty richness of sun-dried tomatoes makes this vegetarian chili full-flavored and robust. If you wish to add meat, try a pound of one of the interesting sausages with sun-dried tomatoes in the filling.

1 lb. dried beans of choice
3 tbs. olive oil
4 anaheim chiles, stemmed and chopped (include seeds)
1 serrano chile, stemmed, seeded and minced
2 cups chopped onions
3 cloves garlic, minced
1 tbs. whole cumin seeds
1 tsp. cayenne pepper
2 cups oil-packed sun-dried tomatoes, coarsely chopped
6 cups chicken broth
1 tbs. dried parsley flakes
1 tbs. crumbled dried oregano
1 tsp. salt
$\frac{1}{2}$ tsp. pepper

Place beans in a large saucepan and cover with water. Bring to a boil over high heat and cook for 5 minutes. Remove from heat and let soak for 1 hour. Rinse and drain.

In a large soup kettle over medium high heat, sauté chiles, onions and garlic until softened. Add cumin and cayenne and stir 1 minute longer. Add tomatoes, broth, seasonings and beans, bring to a boil and reduce heat. Cover and simmer for 2 hours or until tender.

Makes 6 servings

GARDEN CHILI

This recipe is a virtual produce stand in a bowl of chili. Feel free to add or delete vegetables as your garden or palate dictates. There's something therapeutic about growing your own vegetables or going to a farmers' market and selecting the beautiful and colorful fresh vegetables, and then preparing them.

1 eggplant, peeled and cut into ¾-inch cubes
1 tbs. salt
½ cup olive oil
2 cups chopped onion
2 zucchini, cut into ½-inch cubes
1 red bell pepper, cut into ½-inch cubes
1 yellow bell pepper, cut into ½-inch cubes
4 cloves garlic, minced

8 fresh plum tomatoes, cut into ½-inch cubes
1 cup water
1 cup chopped parsley
½ cup chopped fresh basil
½ cup chopped fresh dill
3 tbs. chili powder
1½ tbs. ground cumin
1 tbs. crumbled dried oregano
salt to taste
½ tsp. red pepper flakes

1½ cups fresh or frozen corn kernels

2 cans (16 oz. each) black beans, rinsed and drained

3 tbs. lemon juice

sour cream, grated Monterey Jack cheese and sliced green onions for garnish

Place cubed eggplant in a strainer, toss it with salt and let it stand for 1 hour. (This rids eggplant of excess moisture and bitterness.) Pat eggplant dry with paper towels.

In a large soup kettle over medium high heat, pour in ¼ cup of the olive oil and cook eggplant until tender. Remove and set aside. Add remaining oil to kettle and sauté onion, zucchini, bell pepper and garlic until softened. Add tomatoes, 1 cup water, ½ cup of the parsley and all seasonings to the pan and cook over low heat for 30 minutes, stirring occasionally. Add corn and black beans and cook for 15 minutes. Taste and correct seasoning. It may need a bit of lemon juice or salt. Serve with sour cream, grated Monterey Jack cheese and sliced green onions.

Makes 8 servings

VEGETARIAN LENTIL CHILI

*The degree of heat in chili is a personal thing, so it is easy to please
a variety of palates by setting out condiments and letting people
choose their own. For those who wish to cool things down, serve
sour cream, yogurt, carrot and celery sticks, flour tortillas and
grated cheese. For those who wish to spice things up, offer hot
salsa, pepper sauce, chopped onions and fresh chiles. Certain foods
seem to have a natural affinity with chili — coleslaw, cornbread,
tortillas, beans and of course, beer!*

4 cups dried lentils
3 cups water
3 cups tomato juice
1 can (16 oz.) whole tomatoes,
  chopped, with juice
1 cup bottled salsa
2 tsp. ground cumin
1 tsp. paprika

½ tsp. thyme
12 garlic cloves, minced
2 cups chopped onion
salt to taste
freshly ground pepper to taste
1 can (6 oz.) tomato paste
2 tbs. balsamic vinegar
red pepper flakes to taste

Place lentils, water and tomato juice in a large soup kettle and bring to a boil over medium high heat. Cover, reduce heat and simmer for 30 minutes. Add tomatoes, salsa, cumin, paprika, thyme, garlic and onion. Stir and bring to a boil, reduce heat and simmer for 1 hour, stir every 15 minutes. Add more water if needed. Add salt, pepper and tomato paste and simmer for 30 minutes. Just before serving, add vinegar and red pepper flakes.

Makes 8 servings

HOMEMADE CHILI POWDER

Vary the types of chile peppers to create your own personal blend.

4 dried hot chile peppers
3 dried ancho chile peppers
1 tbs. cumin seeds
1 tsp. garlic powder

1 tsp. ground coriander
1 tsp. crumbled dried oregano
½ tsp. whole cloves

Remove stems and seeds from peppers and cut into small pieces. With a blender or mini food processor, grind ingredients into a fine powder. Store in an airtight container in a cool, dry place.

Makes ⅓ cup

MICROWAVED TORTILLA CUPS FOR CHILI

It's more fun to eat chili when it's served in a tortilla cup.

8-inch flour tortillas

Press tortillas into 10 oz. custard cups. Microwave on HIGH for 2 to 3 minutes. Carefully lift tortillas out of cups and cool on a wire rack.

Makes 8

CHILI SALAD

This recipe is almost like a taco salad. It stretches that last bit of homemade chili and also makes a lighter meal.

6 cups shredded lettuce
3 cups homemade chili, warmed
¾ cup sour cream
¼ cup mayonnaise
1 tomato, seeded and chopped

¼ cup chopped fresh cilantro
6 oz. shredded cheddar cheese
1 red bell pepper, cut into strips
¼ cup sliced ripe olives
¼ cup sliced green onions

Place a bed of greens on each salad plate. Top with chili. With a blender or food processor, combine sour cream, mayonnaise, tomato and cilantro until blended. Drizzle dressing in a zig-zag pattern over chili. Top each serving with cheese, arrange pepper strips on top and scatter with olives and green onions.

Makes 6 servings

EASY CHILI DIP

*This recipe is so easy it's embarrassing! Using your own homemade
chili certainly helps it disappear in a hurry, but commercially canned
chili works too. Serve with plenty of tortilla chips for dipping.*

2 cups chili
8 oz. cream cheese, softened
1 can (4 oz.) diced green chiles

Combine ingredients in a microwave-safe dish, such as a quiche
dish. Heat until bubbly, about 1 to 2 minutes.

Makes 8 servings

CHIPS AND CHILI PIE

This makes a nice family dinner, kind of like a Mexican lasagna.
Homemade chili is best, but you can use canned if you're in a hurry.
Use small tortilla chips or crush larger tortilla chips.

6 cups tortilla chips
4 cups shredded cheese,
  Monterey Jack and cheddar
8 cups chili con carne with beans
1 cup chopped onion

1 can (4 oz.) diced green chiles
salsa, chopped tomatoes,
  shredded lettuce, sour cream
  and sliced black olives for
  garnish

Layer 4 cups of chips in a 9-x-13-inch baking pan. Sprinkle with half the cheese and then top with all of the chili. Top with onion and diced chiles. Add a layer of remaining chips and cheese. Bake at 350° for 25 to 30 minutes or until bubbly. Let stand for 5 minutes to make it easier to serve. Pass garnishes as desired.

Makes 8 servings

CHILI BURRITOS

*This recipe is just a guideline — make your burritos
as original and varied as you want.*

8 flour tortillas, 8-inch diameter, room temperature
8 cups homemade chili
2 cups shredded Monterey Jack or cheddar cheese
½ cup pickled jalapeño chiles, cut into thin rounds
2 cups shredded romaine lettuce
salsa and sour cream

Heat oven to 400°. Place ½ cup of chili in the center of each tortilla, leaving a 2- to 3-inch border around edges. Sprinkle each with ¼ cup cheese and top with jalapeños as desired. Fold each side towards the center and roll ends over. Wrap each burrito tightly in foil. Place on a rimmed baking sheet and bake for 20 minutes. Remove foil and serve with salsa and sour cream.

Makes 8 servings

CHILI SLOPPY JOES

Everyone seems to enjoy sloppy joes. Try this interesting version or any other chili recipe you might wish to try.

3 tbs. vegetable oil
1 cup chopped onion
1 clove garlic, minced
2 tbs. chili powder
1 tsp. crumbled dried oregano
1 tsp. ground cumin
1 tsp. salt

2 lb. lean ground beef
1½ cups tomato salsa
½ cup water
1 can (10½ oz.) dark red kidney beans, rinsed and drained
6 kaiser rolls or hamburger buns
6 slices cheddar cheese, optional

Heat oil in a large skillet. Sauté onion and garlic until softened. Add seasonings and ground beef. Cook until browned and crumbly. Drain off excess juices. Add salsa, water and beans. Brown buns under the broiler. Arrange cheese slices on bun tops and set bottoms on serving plates. Return tops to broiler until cheese begins to melt. Spoon chili mixture onto bottoms of buns and cover with tops.

Makes 6 servings

CHILI FLAVORS

CHILI TACOS

This recipe for a crowd features an interesting taste twist with corn and green olives in the meat mixture. Start marinating the meat at least 2 days before you plan to serve this dish.

¼ cup chili powder
6 cloves garlic, minced
5 tbs. lime juice
3 tbs. olive oil
1 tbs. ground cumin
2½ lb. boneless lean stewing
 beef, cut into 1-inch cubes
1 can (28 oz.) plum tomatoes,
 drained and chopped
2 cups beef broth
12 oz. beer
3 tbs. olive oil
1 cup chopped onion

2 jalapeño chiles, stemmed,
 seeded and minced
1 pkg. (10 oz.) frozen corn,
 thawed
1 cup sliced pimiento-stuffed
 green olives
salt and pepper to taste
20 taco shells or tortillas
12 oz. cheddar cheese, shredded
3 tomatoes, diced
½ head lettuce, shredded
salsa and sour cream for garnish

Combine chili powder, garlic, lime juice, 3 tbs. olive oil and cumin in a large glass bowl to form a marinade. Add beef cubes and mix until coated. Refrigerate overnight, stirring occasionally.

Heat oven to 350°. Combine beef with marinade, tomatoes, broth and beer in a Dutch oven. Bring to a boil on top of the stove over high heat, cover and place in oven. Bake for 45 minutes, uncover and continue to cook 45 minutes longer. Cool beef and shred; return to cooking liquid. Refrigerate overnight.

Heat 3 tbs. olive oil in a heavy skillet over medium heat. Add onion and jalapeños and sauté until tender. Mix in beef mixture, corn, olives, salt and pepper. Bring to a boil, and stirring constantly, cook for 5 minutes. Spoon meat mixture into taco shells; top with cheese, lettuce and tomatoes. Serve with sour cream and salsa.

Makes 20 servings

CHILI POTATO SALAD

*This is something different for true chili lovers. Best of all, it's low in
cholesterol and can be served chilled or at room temperature.*

4 cups sliced cooked red-
  skinned potatoes
1 pkg. (10 oz.) frozen corn,
  thawed
½ cup sliced celery
½ cup chopped red onion
½ cup chopped red bell pepper
½ cup chopped green bell pepper

¼ cup chopped parsley
3 tbs. vegetable oil
¼ cup cider vinegar
2 tsp. chili powder
2 cloves garlic, minced
½ tsp. Tabasco Sauce
salt and pepper

In a large serving bowl, combine potatoes and vegetables. Using a
blender or a food processor, combine oil, vinegar and seasonings. Pour
over vegetables and stir to coat well. Season to taste with salt and
pepper. Cover and refrigerate for up to 2 hours. Serve cold or at room
temperature.

Servings: 6

CHILI MUFFINS

This makes a great Saturday lunch or week night dinner.

4 slices bacon, diced
1 cup chopped onion
1 cup chopped green bell pepper
2 cans (16 oz. each) red kidney
  beans, rinsed and drained
1 can (8 oz.) tomato sauce
1 tbs. chili powder

½ tsp. salt
¼ tsp. pepper
½ lb. cheddar cheese, shredded
6 frankfurters, sliced
6 English muffins, halved and
  toasted

In a large skillet over medium high heat, cook bacon until crisp. Remove bacon and drain on paper towels. In bacon drippings, cook onion and green pepper until soft, but not brown. Add beans, tomato sauce, chili powder, salt and pepper. Stir until heated through. Add reserved bacon, frankfurters and cheese; stir until cheese melts. Spoon over toasted English muffin halves.

Makes 6 servings

CHILI CHICKEN CHUNKS

Serve this appetizer with dips — salsa, salsa mixed with sour cream, and guacamole.

3 whole chicken breasts, skinned, boned and cut into 1-inch chunks
¾ cup flour
¼ cup cornmeal
2 tsp. chili powder
1 tsp. garlic powder
1 tsp. salt

½ tsp. paprika
½ tsp. ground cumin
½ tsp. pepper
¾ cup beer
oil for frying
dips of choice

In a mixing bowl, stir together dry ingredients with a fork. Whisk in beer and make a smooth batter. Add chicken chunks and stir to coat. In a large skillet, pour oil ½-inch deep. Heat over medium high heat. Add chicken pieces to oil one at a time. Do not crowd. Cook until golden brown and cooked through. Remove to a cookie sheet lined with paper towels and keep warm in a low oven while frying remaining chicken. Serve warm with dips.

Makes 8 servings

CHICKEN SALAD WITH GREEN CHILE DRESSING

Serve this colorful salad with hot cornbread for a complete meal.

4 qt. rinsed, torn leaf lettuce
2 cups diced cooked chicken
½ cup thinly sliced red onion
1 cucumber, thinly sliced

2 grapefruits, peeled and sliced
2 avocados, peeled and sliced
¼ cup toasted pine nuts
Green Chile Dressing

Place lettuce in a large shallow salad bowl. Add chicken, onion, cucumber, grapefruit and avocado. Pour *Green Chile Dressing* over salad and toss gently. Sprinkle with pine nuts.

GREEN CHILE DRESSING

1 can (4 oz.) diced green chiles
⅓ cup lime juice
¼ cup chopped cilantro
¼ cup water
1 clove garlic, minced

1 jalapeño chile, stemmed,
  seeded and minced
1½ tsp. sugar
salt to taste

With a blender or food processor, combine ingredients until smooth.

Makes 6 entrée servings; 1 cup dressing

INDEX